Hilarious Children

True Tales of Funny Kid's Experiences

Leroy Vincent

Copyright © 2016. All rights reserved.

No part of this publication may be reproduced, stored in a retrieval system or transmitted in any way by any means, electronic, mechanical, photocopy, recording or otherwise, without the prior permission of the author except as provided by USA copyright law.

All characters appearing in this work are fictitious. Any resemblance to real persons, living or dead, is purely coincidental.

The opinions expressed by the author are not necessarily those of Revival Waves of Glory Books & Publishing.

Published by Revival Waves of Glory Books & Publishing

PO Box 596 I Litchfield, Illinois 62056 USA

www.revivalwavesofgloryministries.com

Revival Waves of Glory Books & Publishing is committed to excellence in the publishing industry.

Book design Copyright © 2016 by Revival Waves of Glory Books & Publishing. All rights reserved.

Published in the United States of America

Paperback: 978-1-68411-214-2

Contents

Story 1 1

Story 2 2

Story 3 4

Story 4 5

Story 5 7

Story 6 8

Story 7 9

Story 8 11

Story 9 12

Story 10 14

Story 11 16

Story 12 18

Story 13 20

Story 14 22

Story 15 23

Story 16 24

Story 17 25

Story 18 27

Story 19 29

Story 20 30

Story 21 32
Story 22 33
Story 23 34
Story 24 35
Story 25 37
Story 26 39
Story 27 40
Story 28 42
Story 29 43
Story 30 44
Story 31 46
Story 32 48
Story 33 50
Story 34 51
Story 35 53
Story 36 54
Story 37 55
Story 38 57
Story 39 59
Story 40 61
Story 41 63

Story 1

A funny baby story I know is when I was helping my best friend, at the time, babysit her little brother. We were not too familiar with babies but had helped her mom out enough that she would go to the store and trust us with the little guy. Well, when we were changing his diaper, we took off his old one and left it way too close to his hands. He grabbed it and threw his little poop all over the room. Us being young, we screamed and ran out of the room which led him to follow us out the door, diaper-less. We couldn't stop laughing at him thinking it was so funny he ran us out of the room. There was a mess to clean up, but it is a classic, funny baby story.

Story 2

When my DD1 was about eleven months old, I was changing her nappy on the floor and putting her pajamas on.

OH's mate was there. He is a really cool guy, who dresses amazingly well, is in a band, and doesn't do relationships or kids etc... He was waiting for OH to get ready because they were going out.

The tab came off the nappy I had so I went to the kitchen to get another one.

OH's mate shouted through to me that DD had crawled off the rug she was lying on.

I asked him to put her back on it because we had tiled floors at the time and she was naked. I got to the living room door just as he picked her up...and she had a diarrhea explosion ALL over him. It was all over his nice jacket, his t-shirt and his jeans. He was in total shock. He just handed DD1 to me and mumbled something about getting changed while I apologized over and over again.

I had to give him some of my OH's clothes to go home in. He still talks about it and DD1 is fifteen now and is mortified when he mentions it.

Story 3

When I was a baby, there was a time when my parents asked my older sister to go in to the next room to check on me and see what I was doing.

My four year old sister went in to the room and reported back to my parents, "He's with the cat". Well, we didn't have a cat!

My parents screamed, "What cat"! So they went in to the next room to find me laughing and playing with a cat. I guess the cat had wandered in from outside and I picked it up and played with it totally un-phased.

They took a great photo and then sent the cat outside on its way.

Story 4

The Ant and the Grasshopper

One summer's day in a field, a grasshopper was hopping about, chirping and singing to its heart's content. An ant passed by, bearing along with great effort an ear of corn he was taking to his bed.

"Why don't you come and chat with me," asked the grasshopper, "instead of toiling your life away?"

"I am helping to store up food for the winter," said the ant, "and I recommend you to do the same."

"Why bother about winter?" said the grasshopper. "We have got plenty of food at present."

Short story but the ant went on its way and continued its toil. When winter came, the grasshopper found itself dying of hunger, while it saw the ants distributing, every day, corn and grain from the stores they had collected in summer. Then the Grasshopper knew...MORAL: WORK TODAY AND YOU CAN REAP THE BENEFITS TOMORROW!

Story 5

For some strange reason yesterday, my little girl wanted us to karate chop the Thanksgiving turkey to smithereens. She kept screaming chop it and doing chopping symbols with her hands. Only when we pretended to beat the crap out of the bird was she satisfied.

Story 6

After I had my first son, via C-section, I felt so alive, vibrant, and blissfully happy. I remember feeling beautiful, gorgeous and radiant in that hospital gown. I gleefully let family take any and all pictures of me. I was on top of the world, in a joy that knew no bounds. This was in the olden days when pictures had to be developed. When I finally saw myself, I saw a bloated, sickly looking person with an ashen pallor and crazy eyes. Yeah, morphine is powerful stuff.

Story 7

When my daughter was two, she was very advanced with her speech. Yes, I was proud of her, and one day I was at the supermarket and pulled a ticket for the queue for some cheese. My DD was in the trolley and tried to tap the lady standing by her. The woman was dripping in expensive clothes and wore a designer coat that was orange with unusual black markings on it.

The woman turned to me and said what a gorgeous little girl I had and that she looked like Shirley Temple - which she did and she said to my DD, 'What do you want lovely? You were tapping my arm, weren't you?'

And DD said, 'You look like a giraffe in that funny coat!'

Omg, I was red as hell! I walked away and hissed at my mother, 'Go and get the trolley......

My mother said, 'Oh God, what's she done now?'

I said, 'Just go and get the trolley! I will tell you later.'

And now my DD is 27 and has three kids of her own and sometimes she says, 'Oh Mum, I was so embarrassed today. Guess what this one said?'

Lol.....oh yes.....I know what's it's like to be an embarrassed Mum!

Story 8

My niece was two months old and she needed some tummy time, to help strengthen her back, shoulder and arm muscles. Well, she was sporting a smattering the beginnings of a diaper rash, so we decided to let her air it out at the same time. Well, all was good for the first five minutes and then it happened. A squirting rainbow of baby poo. It was a perfect arc that landed on the carpet, two feet away from her little bottom. Luckily my brother-in-law was still at work, so my sister in a fit of hysterics, and giggle fest set about cleaning up the carpet and the baby. Sufficed to say that was the last time my niece had free girl tummy time.

Story 9

When I was little, my mom would leave me with my younger brother to watch television. We are nine years apart so I was too young to really bother paying attention to him often. One time, my mom left us to watch television while she did the laundry. When she came back, she sat to watch with us for a little bit. My brother was in his play pen and he was facing the television. My mother sat on the couch behind the play pen so she could only see my brother's back. After a while my brother made a squeaking noise. I looked over at him and saw that his face was completely brown. I screamed and my mom looked over at him. We both realized that he had been playing with his own poop. He had smeared it all over the bottom of the play pen. He had gotten it all over his tiny body. However, worst of all was that he had gotten it all over his face. He looked as if he had done some face painting to look brown. My mom and I spent the next hour bathing him and cleaning the disaster he had made.

Story 10

When I first came home from the hospital with my baby, I learned that he loved music. Music makes him laugh when he is sad. Music helps him relax when he is sleepy. He likes to bounce to the beat on his little baby feet. I started doing the Patty Cake song to get him to stop crying. He loved the Patty Cake song so much he began to clap to and forgot he was upset. I began to do the Patty Cake song every time he got upset. As a result of this practice, every time he gets upset now he claps his hands together to let me know. He is very afraid of strangers but they think he wants to play because he starts to clap. When he is hungry, he claps his hands together. When he gets a boo boo, he claps his hands. When the baby is hungry, he claps his hands. The funny thing is it still makes him happy so he is soothing himself. Sometimes I hear him cry in the middle of the night. A short time later, I will hear him clapping his hands and then laughing. I think he is the funniest little baby and too adorable.

Story 11

As a new mom, I wanted to make sure that I was protecting the baby and taking care of her properly. This included diapering, in which I wanted to make sure she didn't get diaper rash. I used baby powder quite liberally when diapering her to keep her skin protected and covered.

My mother-in-law was quite thrilled to have her first grandchild. She was especially happy it was a girl, since she had three boys and no daughters herself. Once the baby arrived, she volunteered to babysit whenever we wanted.

I had a huge baby shower with lots of relatives, and received lots of diapering products, including lotions, disposable and cloth diapers, diaper wipes, the works. So I thought I had become an expert at diapering when my mother-in-law arrived for her first visit with the baby.

Unfortunately the baby was being fussy and crying when I brought her in the room. My mother-in-law sat on the couch and said it was no problem, she knew how to soothe a fussy baby. She held her against her chest with the baby's head on her shoulder and gently patted the baby's diapered bottom. Suddenly, a huge cloud of baby powder erupted from the sides of the baby's diaper, sending a big cloud into my mother-in-law's face and making her choke and cough. I sheepishly grinned and said, "I guess I used a little too much baby powder!"

Story 12

Okay, so when I was a little kid, maybe two or three years old, my mom asked me a question. She asked me to count to ten and I did. Then she told me to count to ten backwards (meaning to count from ten to one), and so I turned around backwards and counted from one to ten!

I have another one, too. When I was even younger, like maybe even two years old, something funny happened in the kitchen. From even being one year old, I had an advanced vocabulary. My mom says that I was standing up in my high chair in the kitchen and she said that I have to be careful or I would fall down.

Then I looked at her, in my diaper, and said, "Possibility."

Isn't that cute?

Story 13

Wheels up – Heels up!

My colleague, Nell Minow, tells the story of her cousin, newly moved to Chicago and was pregnant with her second child.

The doctor assured her that she would not be delivering soon and it was fine for her husband to leave for a three day trip to London. As she and her toddler watched the plane take off from O'Hare, she went into labor.

She called the only person she knew in Chicago, her brother-in-law; to pick up the toddler and drive her to the hospital and between contractions she called the airline to try to find someone who could get a message to her husband.

Halfway across the Atlantic, he was handed a message from the captain. The airline was great —

as soon as he got to Heath Row they put him on a return flight.

Halfway across the Atlantic for the second time in eight hours, he received another note from the captain, this time with a small bottle of champagne. It said, "It's a boy."

The next time she got pregnant, he did not leave her side.

Story 14

While I was pregnant with my second child, my two and a half year old daughter grabbed some balloons that were lying there and stuffed them in her shirt and looked at me and with a big smile said, "Look Mom, I look like you!" She wouldn't take out the balloons from her shirt and walked around with these giant fake boobs for a long time.

Story 15

Living on a far, we have many closed bad radios so that we are easily able to communicate with each other. Well, it just so happens that we have one in the room next to my child, and one night while putting her to bed and reading a bedtime story the radio went off. It was no big deal, just someone asking for a truck to dump grain into, but my daughter, who was only four at the time, shot straight up half asleep from bed, and goes, "Mom, something talks in here," while hazily looking around the room for the noise.

Story 16

A funny story is one morning when my baby boy woke up and he was screaming and laughing because he was trying to catch mine and his daddy's attention. Once we both woke up, he came near us and smiled so big. A little after that happened, he started laughing because he was pooping. When we checked him to change his diaper, he left a huge mark behind. His entire pajama was stained with poop.

Story 17

Big Frank was having his hair styled at the hairdresser's when a lorry smashed into a car, outside. Draped in a cape, his hair divided with aluminum clips, Frank, an ex-paratrooper corporal, raced out to the car and found the driver unhurt.

The lorry driver, however, was slumped over the wheel, unconscious. Big Frank lost no time in applying his army acquired CPR techniques, including mouth-to-mouth resuscitation. The lorry driver recovered consciousness several times, but kept passing out again.

Soon the ambulance arrived with the paramedics and took over, and Frank returned to his barber's seat. 'I just don't understand why he kept passing out,' he said to the hairdresser. 'I did everything they taught me.'

'Well, put yourself in the lorry driver's place,' said the hairdresser. 'He's driving down the street without a care in the world. The next thing he knows, he's waking up to see some big guy in a green cape with a head full of wires pounding on his chest and kissing him. You'd pass out too.'

Story 18

Kids have their own ways of being funny. My son, who is seven years old, was once given homework to prepare a few lines on "Say No to Crackers" for the school activity as Diwali Festival was approaching soon.

My son loves crackers (though he cracks them moderately only). When I tried helping him prepare these lines for the activity, he refused to memorize them saying that I am going against my own principles of telling him to never lie to anyone in life. He said since he loves crackers, he would not prepare any lines for such an activity.

Later, when the activity happened in the class, he spoke as "I love crackers and hence, I cannot lie and say that I will say no to crackers". The class teacher as well as his entire class was amused and had quite a hearty laugh and later on told me about it.

Besides this, there was another incidence. Once, my son was going down the staircase. As soon as he reached the ground floor, the floor was empty and he slipped. To hold himself from slipping, he held hands with another girl who was standing there and playing. While my son could not save himself from falling, the poor girl slipped and fell along with him. Was quite a funny sight to watch as they both went "bang" on the floor together.

Story 19

Kids and Food

My son was in the backseat of the car and he was eating raisins. I was driving and not paying attention, and I heard him start to yell "Get Out, Get Out!!!" He had put the raisin in his nose and could not get it out. I had to pull over and help get it out. They then thought he was really funny!

Story 20

I have a two-year-old son. He really says the funniest things. Once he says something hilarious, we ask him to repeat it and he says, "No", or he will repeat it.

Today, he went number on his own and I was terrified he went on the floor somewhere. He actually went in the toilet. I was ecstatic.

We get to the drug store for his sister. He says, "Lollipop."

The pharmacist laughs.

I say to him, "How do you know you get a lollipop here?"

He replies, "Lollipop."

And guess what? The pharmacist puts three in the bag. I'm like, 'Well.'

My son is playing on my mom's tablet and it dies. He says to his sister, "I want mommy phone."

I say to myself, 'Well, once he can go to the bathroom on his own, he thinks he can have what he wants.' Ha!

He keeps repeating that he wants my phone then we go get their dad and he says, "Hey daddy, lollipop."

I tell his dad. He just laughs at him. David crosses his arms like he has an attitude at two years old and says under his breath, "Lollipop."

Meanwhile, he hasn't finished the lollipop he has had for 30 minutes.

Story 21

My three-year stuck out her hand and said, "Look at the fly I killed, Mommy."

Since she was eating a juicy pickle at the time, I thrust her contaminated hands under the faucet and washed them with antibacterial soap.

After sitting her down to finish her pickle, I asked, with a touch of awe, "How did you kill that fly all by yourself?"

Between bites, she said, "I hit it with my pickle."

I could not stop laughing.

Story 22

My cousin was nine when my aunt adopted her. She fit into the family instantly and it feels as though we've always had her.

During the first year, she got into a fight with her mom (my aunt.) The next few nights my aunt kept waking up freezing and could not figure out why. It turns out that my nine year old cousin was turning the heat down and also unplugging my aunt's heating blankets.

She called it her "paybacks."

Story 23

Once, when my son was two years old and was potty training, I bought him a potty seat that goes on top of the regular toilet seat with a little cushion with Spiderman on it. He was very interested in his new item he thought was a toy. So I let him play with it as it was new and clean, to get familiar with it in hopes to make toilet training go smooth. Minutes after giving him his potty seat, I had to take a call and was momentarily distracted. As I heard my son start to cry, I seen he had put his potty seat over his head and turned it sideways making it hard to take back off. I think he will remember that as the worst hat ever.

Story 24

My brother in law has one kid who is three years old but very smart and mischievous. As the kid must have noticed that his parents are talking on their phone every day, he also started showing interest. Every time when he sees his Mom attending the phone, he would immediately rush to her and try to take it away from her hands. He always tries the same incident on his Dad when he is talking on his cellphone.

It looks so funny sometimes. So now his father has bought him a toy dummy smartphone for the kid to keep him quiet and occupied but still he insists on the very phone which his Mom and Dad uses as if he has realized that the phone given to him by his parents is not a genuine one. Now the kid's parents are also very confused how to make him quiet and happier. I think this generation's kids are very smart and have more intelligence than previous generation's kids. This generation's kids are more tech savvy and simply love using it whether they know how to operate or not. They are highly addicted to it. Just imagine what future lies ahead of this kid who is only three years old and loves all the tech gadgets. By the time he grows up a little, he would have learned all the skills of using computers, laptops, tablets, smartphones and other tech related products.

Story 25

Some funny and interesting things children do is play the role of adults. They dress like us, girls even make up like their mothers, and some of them look so funny when they sing in the mirror like their favorite singer. Once, I caught my daughter when she was like five years old singing Barney's show songs in front of the mirror. That was so hilarious, and the gestures and the preparation she made of her costume were priceless.

Another thing she used to do in a very, very funny way was falling asleep while eating in her high chair. Once, we were having soup for supper and she was very little. We were quietly eating and because of that she started to get bored, although she was eating a lot. She started yawning and yawning, and then she began to fall asleep until she placed her cheek right in her bowl of soup. She woke up suddenly and instead of crying, she started to laugh.

Story 26

When my son was a preschooler, he used to mash words together or change them completely. We always said we should write them down. The two most clear are when his belly hurts and he told me he had a stummyache (combo of stomach and tummy). The other is when my husband had congestive heart failure. When someone asked me how his dad was, he told them he had a heat fart.....his combo of heart and failure.

Story 27

Kids like to learn new things and they love animals. A funny thing that they do is making the sounds that animal do. For example like cow, horse, cat and chicken.

Kids love to say things that their parents or adults say for example: saying baby to mom just because daddy says so.

Kids also like to play in the dirt when they are toddlers and they put everything in their mouth and this is really funny.

Kids like to stay naked, sometimes in front of the guests.

Kids try to be strong and lift things they can't and it's funny when they get nervous about it.

When a person gives lemon to kids, it is funny because they make a funny face and their body shakes.

Kids draw funny pictures of people or animals or flowers.

When little kids try to sing songs, they raise their voice too loud.

It's funny when kids cry about unreasonable things like "Who ate my ice cream?" when they ate it.

Story 28

Once I asked my brother to tell a fruit name which is red in color.

He answered, "Apple."

I appreciated him and asked him to tell another fruit name which is red in color. He answered, "Another Apple."

Once, my sister and I went to a zoo. There was a lion which was in a glass cage. The lion was roaring and showing its willingness to eat her. But my sister also roared and she enjoying seeing the lion. It was so funny to see that.

Story 29

My little sister was at the doctor's office for her annual checkup. She had to be somewhere around three years old.

The nurse was asking all the standard coordination type questions – touch your nose; put your hands up, jump, etc. Being a healthy capable little devil, she's doing everything fine.

Then, the nurse says, "Stand on one foot."

My little sister looks at the nurse, looks down, and hesitates. Then she walks over and stands on one of the nurse's feet.

Story 30

Many years ago, when my daughter was very young, we were looking at a new house to buy We all had a tour of the house; lounge, kitchen, back garden, garage, upstairs to four bedrooms and a bathroom, then downstairs to see the bathroom downstairs.

It was a sunny and warm day, so we were there quite a while, and were given drinks and chatted to the occupants that wanted to sell the house. We discussed many things about the area, the people, clubs, schools, buses, shops, neighbors, etc...

First, we sat in the garden, and then later we sat in the kitchen. As it grew later in the day, our young daughter started to get bored. We hadn't realized how long we had been there. We had been there over an hour, nearly two.

We left the house, and started talking in the front garden. When we were all there talking, the next door neighbor walked passed. They said, 'Hello.'

My daughter spoke up and asked, "Is that a granddad?"

And we all silently smiled and laughed together so the neighbor did not hear us. When, in fact the granddad was a grandma. We all still laugh about it now. It is a day we will not let her forget even though they have now moved away.

Story 31

Here's a funny story that my nephew did was about ten years ago. He was not even one but he was very advanced for his age. He talked, walked and did everything before the average age.

One day, we were at the mall with his dad and we were looking to buy my nephew's mom a Christmas present. The mall was very busy with people almost touching one another as they passed by.

My nephew saw a grown woman that I guess he thought she was pretty. As she passed by, he smacked her on the butt. The lady turned around in shock and assumed that my nephew's dad did it. Because why would a tiny baby do something like that. I was almost on the floor laughing.

Another funny story about a funny baby is about my daughter. When she was tiny - just a few months old - she would always scream bloody murder at a certain time every day. I would get out of the shower and check on her and every day she would scream. I couldn't figure out why.

Until one day, I didn't take my shower at my regular time. I took it early in the morning instead of in the evening. And what do you know she started screaming, Turns out she was completely terrified of my wet hair. So after figuring that out, I would wait until she was asleep in bed for the night to take my showers.

Story 32

My son's 5th birthday was coming up and he LOVED the Hulk. We were going to have him a big party at home over the weekend but I had decided to take cupcakes to his kindergarten class also on his actual birthday.

As we headed to the deli to get the cupcakes he started screaming, "I WANT HULK NAPKINS!" "I WANT HULK PLATES!" "I WANT GREEN ICE CREAM!"

And I kept saying, "We are having a Hulk birthday over the weekend. We can't afford two big parties. We are here to get cupcakes ONLY, and I can't afford two parties." Again and again I told him how I couldn't afford it.

The day came to take the cupcakes to school and that night his teacher called me. She was laughing almost uncontrollably and said, "I don't mean to embarrass you but this is too good not to share." She proceeds to tell me, "At the end of the day, I set the cupcakes at each desk and then had the class sing happy birthday to Logan." She said Logan was sitting there pouting and she could tell he wasn't happy about something when all of a sudden another little boy stood up and screamed "I HATE CUPCAKES! WHY DIDN'T YOUR MOM GET A CAKE?"

She said Logan shot up out of his desk, walked over to the other boy and shoved him down in his seat screaming, "MY MAMA COULDN'T AFFORD A CAKE, SO JUST SIT DOWN, SHUT UP AND EAT YOUR DAMN CUPCAKE!"

He is twenty-two now and every year on his birthday I still get him a Hulk cupcake to go along with the cake that I can afford now!

Story 33

I was at the beach with a friend and her little boy. I believe he was about two years old at the time. He was running along the water line, when all of a sudden, he fell down and face-planted right in the sand. He immediately began to cry these crocodile tears, and my friend got up and ran over to him. She scooped him up and hugged him tight. He was still crying, but all of a sudden he stopped crying and he looked over at me and gave me this look of an evil villain who's just tricked the hero. Then he began crying again. I'll never forget that look. He had my friend so wrapped around his little finger, and she had no idea.

Story 34

I was helping my sister work in church Sunday school. The kids were always wild and seemed to be hyper early in the morning. These kids were ages 6-7 so there wasn't much learning going on. There were these two twin brothers who were always wild. They would play off of each other and it always seemed they wanted to be the center of attention.

One day, we can't find one of the twins. He's gone. We were going to play a game and we had no idea where he was. We asked his brother but he says he does not know. We call his name, no luck. We are telling him we will have to call his parents from the service. We see the brother start to smile then. He goes to the closet, opens up the door and there is his brother with $20 in his hand; the money their parents gave for church. He had paid his bother to hid and worry us, so funny.

Sometimes kids can be so bad, I feel bad for their parents. I have never seen two brothers play off of each other like these twins did. It was very interesting the connection they had.

Story 35

Tonight, my three year old son was on the potty.

Well, my five year old decided he needed some encouragement. He inched forward so my daughter looked into the toilet and saw a poop and goes, "You are doing great. You already got one, keep on going." Every time she heard a plop, she would said, "Yay! Good Job!"

He would respond, "Yay! I did it! Mommy, are you happy?"

Story 36

Zhu Zhu Pets were some of the most popular toys of the year awhile back. Super hard to find on store shelves! We got our daughter some because I travel a lot and found them in various stores. She never even played with them! Sometimes just because it's popular, doesn't mean everyone wants one, I guess!

Story 37

One time, I was working at a childcare center, and one child was continually misbehaving. Myself, along with other members of the staff, repeatedly had to say, "Connor, what were the directions?"

We re-directed him multiple times to prevent him from accidentally hurting himself or another child.

A different child, a five-year-old, kept overhearing us talk to Connor about his behavior. In the middle of working on a painting, the five year old walked over and casually mentioned to me, "Connor likes to go to jail."

Thinking I misheard what he had said, I asked him to repeat what he told me. He again said, "Connor likes to go to jail."

At this point, I was thinking maybe Connor was his mom's ex-boyfriend or he had a crazy cousin named Connor who was in trouble. I asked him if he knew who Connor was. He said that yes he did, and nonchalantly added, "That's the baby in my mom's tummy. He likes to go to jail."

The five-year-old then walked away and continued his painting. When I looked over at his painting, I noticed that he was painting a picture of his family, including a stick figure mom with a bubble stomach to signify her pregnancy.

Story 38

So one time, I was at my friends and my god daughter was running around the house. She was being a silly girl.

Her mom (my best friend) went outside and my god daughter started freaking out. She wanted to be with her mom but it was too cold for her to go outside.

So the only way I could get her attention was by putting a bucket on my head and chasing after her. She was laughing like a crazy person the whole time. We did circles around the coffee table, out to the kitchen, and back to the coffee table and finally I caught her and picked her up.

She then took the bucket off my head and put it on her head she looked so funny. This silly funny little girl wanted to chase me. So, I put her down and as soon as I did she went running full speed into the book shelf. I panicked but she was laughing and had a huge smile on her face. Thankfully, that bucket saved her from smashing her head into the bookshelf and when her mom came back in she showed her the new bucket on the head trick.

Story 39

My son, Zackary, is three years old. He's been a comedian since birth. He has always gotten sarcasm and always had a sense of humor.

Recently, when it was cold and snowy, I said to him, "I don't like snow."

He responded, "I like snow."

I said, "I don't like cold."

He responded, "I like cold."

I said, "Zackary, you're so contrary."

He responded, "Mommy, I'm not contrary, you are contrary."

Now, he's also started blaming his brother and others for things, for instance, passing gas or bowel movements. If he has an accident, he says, "Mommy, daddy pooped his pants."

My son is also tall and thin. He likes to jump in puddles and today he jumped in puddles at school. His teacher changed him into pants I had in his bag that were a little big on him. I picked him up from school and headed to the car. Just as he arrived at the car, his pants fell down to his ankles leaving him standing there half naked. He turned around, laughed, and told me, "Mommy, it's a full moon."

He has an obsession with using the word poop and butt and frequently swaps words in common children's songs out with poop. We went to a Pittsburgh Pirate's game (also known as the Bucks). As we chanted, "Let's go Bucks", he chanted, "Let's go Butt cheeks."

Story 40

My kids keep me in stitches. When my daughter was about nine, she stumbled into the kitchen and came out with a very concerned look on her face. She ever so seriously asked me what was wrong with the trash can. Puzzled, it took me a few minutes to realize she was holding TRASH in her hand and I had to inform her that the trashcan was not broken, I had just taken the bag full of trash out and forgot to fill it with a fresh bag!

Then just last week, I told her to wash the dishes. Keep in mind that I use my dishwasher as a drying rack as I hand wash most of the time. So my kids are used to always grabbing a dish clean from the dishwasher. She washed a sink full of dishes, loaded them in the dishwasher and turned it on. Confused, I asked why she would run the dishwasher after hand washing and she very matter of factly told me that since that's how I do it, she wanted to do it right. Can't fault her I guess?

Story 41

My son sleepwalks and pees on the kitchen floor. Luckily, it's always about the time I don't feel like mopping the floor AGAIN!

My youngest daughter? She may be insane. She walks around asking EVERYONE when they're having their baby. Literally EVERYONE. This kid can have you doing crunches all night.

Other Books By Leroy Vincent

Finding Your Match

Fun Dog Days

Fun Dog Days Coloring Book

Funny Cat Stories

Heartbreak Hotel

Hilarious Children

Romance Regrets

Christmas Coloring Pages

Mystic Elves Coloring Pages

www.ingramcontent.com/pod-product-compliance
Lightning Source LLC
Chambersburg PA
CBHW052117070526
44584CB00017B/2522